GILLIAN CLARKE was born in Cardiff [...] Ceredigion. A poet, writer, playright [...] Creative Writing at the University of Glamorgan, she is also president of Ty Newydd, the writers' centre in North Wales which she co-founded in 1990. Carcanet publish her *Collected Poems* and *Selected Poems*.

Also by Gillian Clarke from Carcanet Press

Collected Poems
The King of Britain's Daughter
Five Fields
Selected Poems
Making the Beds for the Dead

GILLIAN CLARKE

Letter from a Far Country

CARCANET

Acknowledgements

Acknowledgement is due to the editors of the following publications in which some of these poems first appeared: *Poetry Wales, Arcade, Poetry Review, The New Statesman, The Honest Ulsterman, Madog, P.N. Review, Pequod, The Chimaera Press, The Kilpeck Anthology* (Five Seasons Press), *Poems for Shakespeare 9, Yr Academi Gymreig / The Welsh Academy.* Acknowledgement is also due to the Welsh Arts Council and BBC Wales for commissioning and broadcasting the title poem.

First published in Great Britain in 1982 by
Carcanet Press Limited
Alliance House
Cross Street
Manchester M2 7AQ

This edition first published 2006

A CIP catalogue record for this book is available from the British Library
ISBN 1 85754 961 9
978 1 85754 961 4

The publisher acknowledges financial assistance from the Arts Council of England

Typeset by XL Publishing Services, Tiverton
Printed and bound in England by SRP Ltd, Exeter

Contents

Letter from a Far Country

They have gone. The silence resettles
slowly as dust on the sunlit
surfaces of the furniture.
At first the skull itself makes
sounds in any fresh silence,
a big sea running in a shell.
I can hear my blood rise and fall.

Dear husbands, fathers, forefathers,
this is my apologia, my
letter home from the future,
my bottle in the sea which might
take a generation to arrive.

The morning's all activity.
I draw the detritus of a family's
loud life before me, a snow plough,
a road-sweeper with my cart of leaves.
The washing machine drones
in the distance. From time to time
as it falls silent I fill baskets
with damp clothes and carry them
into the garden, hang them out,
stand back, take pleasure counting
and listing what I have done.
The furniture is brisk with polish.
On the shelves in all of the rooms
I arrange the books
in alphabetical order
according to subject: Mozart,
Advanced Calculus, William,
and Paddington Bear.
Into the drawers I place your clean
clothes, pyjamas with buttons
sewn back on, shirts stacked neatly
under their labels on the shelves.

The chests and cupboards are full,
the house sweet as a honeycomb.
I move in and out of the hive
all day, harvesting, ordering.
You will find all in its proper place,
When I have gone.

As I write I am far away.
First see a landscape. Hill country,
essentially feminine,
the sea not far off. Its blues
widen the sky. Bryn Isaf
down there in the crook of the hill
under Calfaria's single eye.
My grandmother might have lived there.
Any farm. Any chapel.
Father and minister, on guard,
close the white gates to hold her.

A stony track turns between
ancient hedges, narrowing,
like a lane in a child's book.
Its perspective makes the heart restless
like the boy in the rhyme, his stick
and cotton bundle on his shoulder.

The minstrel boy to the war has gone.
But the girl stays. To mind things.
She must keep. And wait. And pass time.

There's always been time on our hands.
We read this perfectly white page
for the black head of the seal,
for the cormorant, as suddenly gone
as a question from the mind,
snaking underneath the surfaces.
A cross of gull shadow on the sea
as if someone stepped on its grave.
After an immeasurable space
the cormorant breaks the surface
as a small, black, returning doubt.

From here the valley is narrow,
the lane lodged like a halfway ledge.
From the opposite wood the birds
ring like a tambourine. It's not
the birdsong of a garden, thrush
and blackbird, robin and finch,
distinguishable, taking turn.
The song's lost in saps and seepings,
amplified by hollow trees,
cupped leaves and wind in the branches.
All their old conversations
collected carefully, faded
and difficult to read, yet held
forever as voices in a well.

Reflections and fallen stones; shouts
into the scared dark of lead-mines;
the ruined warehouse where the owls stare;
sea-caves; cellars; the back stairs
behind the chenille curtain;
the landing when the lights are out;
nightmares in hot feather beds;
the barn where I'm sent to fetch Taid;
that place where the Mellte flows
boldly into limestone caves
and leaps from its hole a mile on,
the nightmare still wild in its voice.

When I was a child a young boy
was drawn into a pipe and drowned
at the swimming pool. I never
forgot him, and pity rivers
inside mountains, and the children
of Hamelin sucked in by music.
You can hear children crying
from the empty woods.
It's all given back in concert
with the birds and leaves and water
and the song and dance of the Piper.

Listen! to the starlings glistening
on a March morning! Just one day
after snow, an hour after frost,
the thickening grass begins to shine
already in the opening light.
There's wind to rustle the blood,
the sudden flame of crocus.

My grandmother might be standing
in the great silence before the Wars.
Hanging the washing between trees
over the white and the red hens.
Sheets, threadworked pillowcases.
Mamgu's best pais, her Sunday frock.

The sea stirs restlessly between
the sweetness of clean sheets,
the lifted arms,
the rustling petticoats.

My mother's laundry list, ready
on Mondays when the van called.
The rest soaked in glutinous starch
and whitened with a bluebag
kept in a broken cup.

(In the airing cupboard you'll see
a map, numbering and placing
every towel, every sheet.
I have charted all your needs.)

It has always been a matter
of lists. We have been counting,
folding, measuring, making,
tenderly laundering cloth
ever since we have been women.

The waves are folded meticulously,
perfectly white. Then they are tumbled
and must come to be folded again.

Four herring gulls and their shadows
are shouting at the clear glass
of a shaken wave. The sea's a sheet
bellying in the wind, snapping.
Air and white linen. Our airing cupboards
are full of our satisfactions.

The gulls grieve at our contentment.
It is a masculine question.
'Where' they call 'are your great works?'
They slip their fetters and fly up
to laugh at land-locked women.
Their cries are cruel as greedy babies.

Our milky tendernesses dry
to crisp lists; immaculate
linen; jars labelled and glossy
with our perfect preserves.
Spiced oranges; green tomato
chutney; seville orange marmalade
annually staining gold
the snows of January.

(The saucers of marmalade
are set when the amber wrinkles
like the sea if you blow it.)

Jams and jellies of blackberry,
crabapple, strawberry, plum,
greengage and loganberry.
You can see the fruit pressing
their little faces against the glass;
tiny onions imprisoned
in their preservative juices.

Familiar days are stored whole
in bottles. There's a wet morning
orchard in the dandelion wine;
a white spring distilled
in elderflower's clarity;
and a loving, late, sunburning

day of October in syrups
of rose hip and the beautiful
black sloes that stained the gin to rose.

It is easy to make of love
these ceremonials. As priests
we fold cloth, break bread, share wine,
hope there's enough to go round.

(You'll find my inventories pinned
inside all of the cupboard doors.)

Soon they'll be planting the barley.
I imagine I see it, stirring
like blown sand, feel the stubble
cutting my legs above blancoed
daps in a summer too hot
for Wellingtons. The cans of tea
swing squeakily on wire loops,
outheld, not to scald myself,
over the ten slow leagues
of the field of golden knives.
To be out with the men, at work,
I had longed to carry their tea,
for the feminine privilege,
for the male right to the field.
Even that small task made me bleed.
Halfway between the flowered lap
of my grandmother and the black
heraldic silhouette of men
and machines on the golden field,
I stood crying, my ankle bones
raw and bleeding like the poppies
trussed in the corn stooks in their torn
red silks and soft mascara blacks.

(The recipe for my best bread,
half granary meal, half strong brown flour,
water, sugar, yeast and salt,
is copied out in the small black book.)

In the black book of this parish
a hundred years ago
you will find the unsupported
woman had 'pauper' against her name.
She shared it with old men.

The parish was rich with movement.
The woollen mills were spinning.
Water-wheels milled the sunlight
and the loom's knock was a heart
behind all activity.
The shuttles were quick as birds
in the warp of the oakwoods.
In the fields the knives were out
in a glint of husbandry.
In back bedrooms, barns and hedges,
in hollows of the hills,
the numerous young were born.

The people were at work:
dressmaker; wool carder; quilter;
midwife; farmer; apprentice;
house servant; scholar; labourer;
shepherd; stocking knitter; tailor;
carpenter; mariner; ploughman;
wool spinner; cobbler; cottager;
Independent Minister.

And the paupers: Enoch Elias
and Ann, his wife; David Jones,
Sarah and Esther their daughter;
Mary Evans and Ann Tanrallt;
Annie Cwm March and child;
Eleanor Thomas, widow, Cryg Glas;
Sara Jones, 84, and daughter;
Nicholas Rees, aged 80, and his wife;
Mariah Evans the Cwm, widow;
on the parish for want of work.
Housebound by infirmity, age,
widowhood, or motherhood.
Before the Welfare State who cared
for sparrows in a hard spring?

The stream's cleaner now; it idles
past derelict mill-wheels; the drains
do its work. Since the tanker sank
the unfolding rose of the sea
blooms on the beaches, wave on wave
black, track-marked, each tide
a procession of the dead.
Slack water's treacherous; each veined
wave is a stain in seal-milk;
the sea gapes, hopelessly
licking itself.

(Examine
your hands scrupulously
for signs of dirt in your own blood.
And wash them before meals.)

In that innocent smallholding
where the swallows live and field mice
winter and the sheep barge in
under the browbone, the windows
are blind, are doors for owls,
bolt-holes for dreams. The thoughts have flown.
The last death was a suicide.
The lowing cows discovered her,
the passing bell of their need
warned a winter morning that day
when no one came to milk them.
Later, they told me, a baby
was born in the room where she died,
as if by this means sanctified,
a death outcried by a birth.
Middle-aged, poor, isolated,
she could not recover
from mourning an old parent's death.
Influenza brought an hour
too black, too narrow to escape.

More mysterious to them
was the woman who had everything.
A village house with railings;
rooms of good furniture;
fine linen in the drawers;
a garden full of herbs and flowers;
a husband in work; grown sons.
She had a cloud on her mind,
they said, and her death shadowed them.
It couldn't be explained.
I watch for her face looking out,
small and white, from every window,
a face in a jar. Gossip,
whispers, lowing sounds. Laughter.

The people have always talked.
The landscape collects conversations
as carefully as a bucket,
gives them back in concert
with a wood of birdsong.

(If you hear your name in that talk
don't listen. Eavesdroppers never
heard anything good of themselves.)

When least expected you catch
the eye of the enemy
looking coldly from the old world.
Here's a woman who ought to be
up to her wrists in marriage;
not content with the second hand
she is shaking the bracelets
from her arms. The sea circles
her ankles. Watch its knots loosen
from the delicate bones
of her feet, from the rope of foam
about a rock. The seal swims
in a collar of water
drawing the horizon in its wake.
And doubt breaks the perfect
white surface of the day.

About the tree in the middle
of the cornfield the loop of gold
is loose as water; as the love
we should bear one another.

When I rock the sea rocks. The moon
doesn't seem to be listening
invisible in a pale sky,
keeping a light hand on the rein.
Where is woman in this trinity?
The mare who draws the load?
The hand on the leather?
The cargo of wheat?

Watching sea-roads I feel
the tightening white currents,
am waterlogged, my time set
to the sea's town clock.
My cramps and drownings, energies,
desires draw the loaded net
of the tide over the stones.

A lap full of pebbles and then
light as a Coca Cola can.
I am freight. I am ship.
I cast ballast overboard.
The moon decides my Equinox.
At high tide I am leaving.

The women are leaving.
They are paying their taxes
and dues. Filling in their passports.
They are paying to Caesar
what is Caesar's, to God what is God's.
To woman what is Man's.

I hear the dead grandmothers,
Mamgu from Ceredigion,
Nain from the North, all calling
their daughters down from the fields,
calling me in from the road.

They haul at the taut silk cords;
set us fetching eggs, feeding hens,
mixing rage with the family bread,
lock us to the elbows in soap suds.
Their sculleries and kitchens fill
with steam, sweetnesses, goosefeathers.

On the graves of my grandfathers
the stones, in their lichens and mosses,
record each one's importance.
Diaconydd. Trysorydd.
Pillars of their society.
Three times at chapel on Sundays.
They are in league with the moon
but as silently stony
as the simple names of their women.

We are hawks trained to return
to the lure from the circle's
far circumference. Children sing
that note that only we can hear.
The baby breaks the waters,
disorders the blood's tune, sets
each filament of the senses
wild. Its cry tugs at flesh, floods
its mother's milky fields.
Nightly in white moonlight I wake
from sleep one whole slow minute
before the hungry child
wondering what woke me.

School's out. The clocks strike four.
Today this letter goes unsigned,
unfinished, unposted.
When it is finished
I will post it from a far country.

★

If we launch the boat and sail away
Who will rock the cradle? Who will stay?
If women wander over the sea
Who'll be home when you come in for tea?

If we go hunting along with the men
Who will light the fires and bake bread then?
Who'll catch the nightmares and ride them away
If we put to sea and we sail away?

Will the men grow tender and the children strong?
Who will teach the Mam iaith and sing them songs?
If we adventure more than a day
Who will do the loving while we're away?

Miracle on St. David's Day

They flash upon that inward eye
Which is the bliss of solitude.
– 'The Daffodils', Wordsworth

An afternoon yellow and open-mouthed
with daffodils. The path treads the sun
among cedars and enormous oaks.
It might be a country house, guests strolling,
the rumps of gardeners between nursery shrubs.

I am reading poetry to the insane.
An old woman, interrupting, offers
as many buckets of coal as I need.
A beautiful chestnut-haired boy listens
entirely absorbed. A schizophrenic

on a good day, they tell me later.
In a cage of first March sun a woman
sits not listening, not seeing, not feeling.
In her neat clothes the woman is absent.
A big, mild man is tenderly led

to his chair. He has never spoken.
His labourer's hands on his knees, he rocks
gently to the rhythms of the poems.
I read to their presences, absences,
to the big, dumb labouring man as he rocks.

He is suddenly standing, silently,
huge and mild, but I feel afraid. Like slow
movement of spring water or the first bird
of the year in the breaking darkness,
the labourer's voice recites 'The Daffodils'.

The nurses are frozen, alert; the patients
seem to listen. He is hoarse but word-perfect.
Outside the daffodils are still as wax,
a thousand, ten thousand, their syllables
unspoken; their creams and yellows still.

Forty years ago, in a Valleys school,
the class recited poetry by rote.
Since the dumbness of misery fell
he has remembered there was a music
of speech and that once he had something to say.

When he's done, before the applause, we observe
the flowers' silence. A thrush sings
and the daffodils are flame.

Insomnia

Afternoon sleeping is best. The fallen book;
sunlight on walls; green leaves
on white curtains are emblematic woods.
The stone-deep drop from consciousness
into cold darkness, till the rope jerks.
The fronded upper reaches are passed,
to a leafless, sunless, soundless dark.

At night I listen to clocks, could walk
the streets, too excited by night
sounds for sleeping, cannot let fall
the book of the mind.

Chalk Pebble

for Jeremy Hooker

The heels of the foetus knead
the stone's roundness out of shape,
downtreading flesh, distorting
the ellipses of the sphere.

It is unexpectedly
salty to touch, its texture
warmer, rougher, weightier
in my hand than I had thought.

Boisterous in its bone
cradle, a stone-breaker,
thief in its mother's orchard.
it is apple-round.

Here the navel
knots it from its chalk down;
there the pressure as the embryo
kicks against ribcage and hip.

The cicatrice of a flower
is printed on one of its
curved surfaces. I carry it
as I walk Glamorgan beaches,

a warm, strange thing to worry
with my fingers. The fossil locked
in its belly stirs, a tender
fresh upheaval of the stone.

Sunday

Getting up early on a Sunday morning
leaving them sleep for the sake of peace,
the lunch pungent, windows open
for a blackbird singing in Cyncoed.

Starlings glistening in the gutter come
for seed. I let the cats in from the night,
their fur already glossed and warm
with March. I bring the milk, newspaper,

settle here in the bay of the window to watch
people walking to church for Mothering Sunday.
A choirboy holds his robes over his shoulder.
The cats jump up on windowsills to wash

and tremble at the starlings. Like peaty water
sun slowly fills the long brown room.
Opening the paper I admit to this
the starved stare of a warning I can't name.

East Moors

At the end of a bitter April
the cherries flower at last in Penylan.
We notice the white trees and the flash
of sea with two blue islands beyond
the city, where the steelworks used to smoke.

I live in the house I was born in,
am accustomed to the sudden glow
of flame in the night sky, the dark sound
of something heavy dropped, miles off,
the smell of sulphur almost natural.

In Roath and Rumney now, washing strung
down the narrow gardens will stay clean.
Lethargy settles in front rooms and wives
have lined up little jobs for men to do.

A few men stay to see it through. Theirs
the bitterest time as rolling mills
make rubble. Demolition gangs
erase skylines whose hieroglyphs
recorded all our stories.

I am reminded of that Sunday
years ago when we brought the children
to watch two water cooling towers
blown up, recall the appalling void
in the sunlight, like a death.

On this first day of May an icy
rain is blowing through this town,
quieter, cleaner, poorer from today.
The cherries are in flower in Penylan.
Already over East Moors the sky whitens, blind.

Scything

It is blue May. There is work
to be done. The spring's eye blind
with algae, the stopped water
silent. The garden fills
with nettle and briar.
Dylan drags branches away.
I wade forward with my scythe.

There is stickiness on the blade.
Yolk on my hands. Albumen and blood.
Fragments of shell are baby-bones,
the scythe a scalpel, bloodied and guilty
with crushed feathers, mosses, the cut cords
of the grass. We shout at each other,
each hurting with a separate pain.

From the crown of the hawthorn tree
to the ground the willow warbler
drops. All day in silence she repeats
her question. I too return
to the place holding the pieces,
at first still hot from the knife,
recall how warm birth fluids are.

Bluetit and Wren

Two of all those
that have lived in our wall
left us their meanings.

The bluetit found
after bitter winter,
yellow feathers

just reachable, blue down
at fingertip, beak turned
to breast as though

the sky that called her
to build among stones froze her
to ammonite.

And the brown wren
who whirred from her cave as I
repeatedly

turned the corner
with a shovel of fresh mortar
for your pointing.

We met there, placed
our fingers in the wren's nest
holding our breath

at mossy heat,
the delicate tiny eggs
each with its pulse.

Such secret interiors.

Llŷr

Ten years old, at my first Stratford play:
The river and the king with their Welsh names
Bore in the darkness of a summer night
Through interval and act and interval.
Swans moved double through glossy water
Gleaming with imponderable meanings.
Was it Gielgud on that occasion?
Or ample Laughton, crazily white-gowned,
Pillowed in wheatsheaves on a wooden cart,
Who taught the significance of little words?
All. Nothing. Fond. Ingratitude. Words
To keep me scared, awake at night. That old
Man's vanity and a daughter's 'Nothing',
Ran like a nursery rhythm in my head.

Thirty years later on the cliffs of Llŷn
I watch how Edgar's crows and choughs still measure
How high cliffs are, how thrown stones fall
Into history, how deeply the bruise
Spreads in the sea where the wave has broken.
The turf is stitched with tormentil and thrift,
Blue squill and bird bones, tiny shells, heartsease.
Yellowhammers sing like sparks in the gorse.
The landscape's marked with figures of old men
The bearded sea; thin-boned, wind-bent trees;
Shepherd and labourer and night-fisherman.
Here and there among the crumbling farms
Are lit kitchen windows on distant hills,
And guilty daughters longing to be gone.

Night falls on Llŷn, on forefathers,
Old Celtic kings and the more recent dead,
Those we are still guilty about, flowers
Fade in jam jars on their graves; renewed
Refusals are heavy on our minds.
My head is full of sound, remembered speech,

Syllables, ideas just out of reach;
The close, looped sound of curlew and the far
Subsidiary roar, cadences shaped
By the long coast of the peninsula,
The continuous pentameter of the sea.
When I was ten a fool and a king sang
Rhymes about sorrow, and there I heard
That nothing is until it has a word.

Blodeuwedd

for Rosie and Susan

Hours too soon a barn owl
broke from woodshadow.
Her white face rose
out of darkness
in a buttercup field.

Colourless and soundless, feathers
cream as meadowsweet
and oakflowers, condemned
to the night, to lie alone
with her sin.

Deprived too of afternoons
in the comfortable sisterhood
of women moving in kitchens
among cups, cloths and running
water while they talk,

as we three talk tonight
in Hendre, the journey over.
We pare and measure and stir,
heap washed apples in a bowl, recall
the day's work, our own fidelities.

Her night lament
beyond conversation,
the owl follows
her shadow like a cross
over the fields,

Blodeuwedd's ballad
where the long reach
of the peninsula
is black in a sea
aghast with gazing.

Siege

I waste the sun's last hour sitting here
at the kitchen window. Tea and a pile
of photographs to sort. Radio news
like smoke of conflagrations far away.
There isn't room for another petal
or leaf out there, this year of blossom.
Light dazzles the hedge roots underneath
the heavy shadows, burns the long grass.

I, in my father's arms in this garden,
with dandelion hair. He, near forty,
unaccustomed to the restlessness
of a baby's energy. Small hands
tear apart the photograph's composure.
She pushes his chest to be let down
where daisies embroider his new shoes.

Perfumes and thorns are tearing
from the red may tree. Wild white morello
and a weeping cherry heavy in flower.
The lilac slowly shows. Small oaks spread
their gestures. Poplars glisten. Pleated green
splits black husks of ash. Magnolia
drops its wax. Forsythia
fallen like a yellow dress.
Underfoot daisies from a deep
original root burst the darkness.

My mother, posing in a summer dress
in the corn at harvest time. Her brothers
shadowy middle distance figures
stoop with pitchforks to lift the sheaves.
Out of sight Captain, or Belle, head fallen
to rest in the lee of the load, patient
for the signal. Out of heart too the scare
of the field far down from the sunstruck top
of the load, and the lurch at the gate
as we ditch and sway left down the lane.

The fallen sun lies low in the bluebells.
It is nearly summer. Midges hang
in the air. A wren is singing, sweet
in a lilac tree. Thrushes hunt the lawn,
eavesdrop for stirrings in the daisy roots.
The wren repeats his message distantly.
In a race of speedwell over grass
the thrushes are silently listening.
A yellow butterfly begins
its unsteady journey over the lawn.

The radio voices break and suddenly
the garden burns, is full of barking dogs.
A woman screams and gunsmoke blossoms
in the apple trees. Sheaves of fire
are scorching the grass and in my kitchen
is a roar of floors falling, machine guns.

The wren moves closer and repeats that song
of lust and burgeoning. Never clearer
the figures standing on the lawn, sharpnesses
of a yellow butterfly, almost there.

Cardiff Elms

Until this summer
through the open roof of the car
their lace was light as rain
against the burning sun.
On a rose-coloured road
they laid their inks,
knew exactly, in the seed,
where in the sky they would reach
precise parameters.

Traffic-jammed under a square
of perfect blue I thirst
for their lake's fingering
shadow, trunk by trunk arching
a cloister between the parks
and pillars of a civic architecture,
older and taller than all of it.

Heat is a salt encrustation.
Walls square up to the sky
without the company of leaves
or the town life of birds.
At the roadside this enormous
firewood, elmwood, the start
of some terrible undoing.

The Water Diviner

His fingers tell water like prayer.
He hears its voice in the silence
through fifty feet of rock
on an afternoon dumb with drought.

Under an old tin bath, a stone,
an upturned can, his copper pipe
glints with discovery. We dip our hose
deep into the dark, sucking its dryness,

till suddenly the water answers,
not the little sound we know,
but a thorough bass too deep
for the naked ear, shouts through the hose

a word we could not say, or spell, or remember,
something like 'Dŵr . . . dŵr'.

Hay-Making

You know the hay's in
when gates hang slack
in the lanes. These hot nights
the fallen fields lie open
under the moon's clean sheets.

The homebound road is
sweet with the liquors
of the grasses, air
green with the pastels
of stirred hayfields.

Down at Fron Felen
in the loaded barn
new bales displace
stale darknesses. Breathe.
Remember finding
first kittens, first love
in the scratch of the hay,
our sandals filled with seeds.

Harvest

Think of our gradual seasons:
those three brothers at their work
turning the pale waves of hay
in the high noon of July;
us at our high moment
with our sheaves of glittering summer,
storing gold as nights turn chill.

Friesian Bull

He blunders through the last dream
of the night. I hear him, waking.
A brick and concrete stall, narrow
as a heifer's haunches. Steel bars
between her trap and his small yard.
A froth of slobbered hay droops
from the stippled muzzle. In the slow
rolling mass of his skull his eyes
surface like fish bellies.

He is chained while they swill his floor.
His stall narrows to rage. He knows
the sweet smell of a heifer's fear.
Remembered summer haysmells reach him,
a trace of the herd's freedom,
clover-loaded winds. Seed
blows up the Dee breathing of plains,
of cattle wading in shallows.
His eyes churn with their vision.

Jac Codi Baw

They have torn down in the space of time
it takes to fill a shopping bag,
the building that stood beside my car.
It was grown over with ragwort,
toadflax and buddleia, windows
blind with boarding. Other cars
had time to drive away. Mine
is splattered with the stones' blood, smoky
with ghosts. We are used to the slow
change that weather brings, the gradual
death of a generation, old bricks
crumbling. Inside the car dust lies,
grit in my eyes, in my hair.

He doesn't care. It's a joke to him
clearing space for the pile-drivers,
cheerful in his yellow machine,
cat-calling, laughing at my grief.
But for him too the hand-writing
of a city will be erased.
I can't laugh. Too much comes down
in the deaths of warehouses. Brickdust,
shards of Caernarfon slate. Blood on our hands

Taid's Funeral

From a drawer, a scrap of creased cloth,
an infant's dress of yellowed Viyella
printed with daisies. And a day opens
suddenly as light. The sun is hot.
Grass grows cleanly to a chapel wall.
The stones are rough as a sheepdog's tongue
on the skin of a two-year child.
They allow a fistful of white
gravel, chain her wrists with daisies.

Under the yew tree they lay Taid
in his box like a corm in the ground.

The lawn-mowers are out. Fears repeat
in a conversation of mirrors,
doll within doll; and that old man too small
at last to see, perfect, distinct as a seed.
My hands are cut by silver gravel.
There are dark incisions in the stalks
of the daisies made by a woman's nail.
A new dress stains green with their sap.

White Roses

Outside the green velvet sitting room
white roses bloom after rain.
They hold water and sunlight
like cups of fine white china.

Within the boy who sleeps in my care
in the big chair the cold bloom
opens at terrible speed
and the splinter of ice moves

in his blood as he stirs awake.
Remembering me he smiles
politely, gritting his teeth
in silence on pain's red blaze.

A stick man in the ashes, his fires
die back. He is spars and springs.
He can talk again, gather
his cat to his bones. She leaps

with a small cry in her throat, kneading
with diamond paws his dry
as tinder flesh. The least spark
of pain will burn him like straw.

The sun carelessly shines after rain.
The cat tracks thrushes in sweet
dark soil. And without concern
the rose outlives the child.

Pendzhikent

A Tadzek boy rides his bicycle in the desert.
Through spokes of his spinning wheels and hundreds of miles
of veils and illusions of bronze air,
mountains are a long white wave unrolling.

They dig for a lost city in the sand.
I can't tell interior from street,
tiled floor from paved way, if an arch
is a door into sand, whether window

looked on light or the dark room of itself.
How do they know structure from dust?
Children finding castles in the sand,
they crack the desert for its fossil.

Their hands are sandals on secret pavements.
Storey by storey they sift dust-drifts
from doorway and sill, from stairs
which step into sand as if it were water.

His bicycle wheel still ticking heat to a blur,
the boy lowers his bucket, withdraws
his share of the desert,
searching the dust for footprints.

Login

Chapel and bridge. A headlong fall
into woods. A river running fast
divides the wild cow parsley.
'My father lived here once,' I said,
'I think you knew him.'

The sun, hot at our backs, whitens
the lane. She, in shadow, allows
the sun to pass her into the passage.
I gain entry at his name, tea,
a lace cloth on the table.

When talking is done she ruffles
my son's brown hair with a hand
that is bruised with age. Veins stand,
fast water in her wrists. Handshakes.
glances converging could not span
such giddy water.

Out in the lane the thrush outsings
the river. The village is at lunch.
The bridge burns with cow parsley.
We stand in the brilliance without words,
watch him running into the light.

Should he turn now to wave and wait
for me, where sunlight concentrates
blindingly on the bridge, he'd see
all this in sepia, hear footsteps
not yet taken fade away.

Blodeuyn

The dark wound in the corn
is a right of way through barley.
The first fine evening after summer floods
we wade waist deep in it.
Pattern of bright barley in my hand
exactly shadowed in deep tyre tracks
that barley-print the mud.

We follow Lloyd in the dusk
through corn into beech trees, a sunken
lane, only the dry risen stones,
white underfoot, to show the way.
Blodeuyn at the dark lane's end,
flowers fallen, as purples fall
from husks of August foxgloves.

A longhouse crouching on the long
white bones of beech trees, empty
sixty years, an animal quiet
in it, of old women stooping
at the door they shared with cattle.
My clogs on cobbles muffle theirs.
Birds scare from the eye sockets.

We turn for home up the muddy fosse,
cross the pale field diagonally.
First stars. The harebell-thin thread
of a distant tree. In the dusk
the moon's delicate skull watches
while we stumble home through smells
of the barley's bowed wet heads,
Blodeuyn's silence in us.

Death of a Cat

His nightmare rocked the house
but no one woke, accustomed
to the heart's disturbances.

We dug a grave last night
under the apple tree where fruit
fattens in green clusters.

Black and white fur perfect
except where soil fell
or where small blood seeped

between the needles of her teeth
in the cracked china of her bones.
Perfect but for darkness

clotting the skull and silence
like the note of an organ
hanging in the locked air.

Dylan dreamed it again,
woken by caterwauling.
Two mourners held a wake

at dawn on the compost heap
(her special place) yowling
to wake the sleeping and to stop

the heart, considering
animal mysteries,
the otherness of pain.

He watched, from the window,
the dawn moon dissolving
its wafer on the tongue.

Sheila na Gig at Kilpeck

Pain's a cup of honey in the pelvis.
She burns in the long, hot afternoon, stone
among the monstrous nursery faces
circling Kilpeck church. Those things we notice
as we labour distantly revolve
outside her perpetual calendar.
Men in the fields. Loads following the lanes,
strands of yellow hair caught in the hedges.

The afternoon turns round us.
The beat of the heart a great tongue in its bell,
a swell between bone cliffs; restlessness
that sets me walking; that second sight
of shadows crossing cornfields. We share
premonitions, are governed by moons
and novenas, sisters cooling our wrists
in the stump of a Celtic water stoup.

Not lust but long labouring
absorbs her, mother of the ripening
barley that swells and frets at its walls.
Somewhere far away the Severn presses,
alert at flood-tide. And everywhere rhythms
are turning their little gold cogs, caught
in her waterfalling energy.

Plums

When their time comes they fall
without wind, without rain.
They seep through the trees' muslin
in a slow fermentation.

Daily the low sun warms them
in a late love that is sweeter
than summer. In bed at night
we hear heartbeat of fruitfall.

The secretive slugs crawl home
to the burst honeys, are found
in the morning mouth on mouth,
inseparable.

We spread patchwork counterpanes
for a clean catch. Baskets fill,
never before such harvest,
such a hunters' moon burning

the hawthorns, drunk on syrups
that are richer by night
when spiders are pitching
tents in the wet grass.

This morning the red sun
is opening like a rose
on our white wall, prints there
the fishbone shadow of a fern.

The early blackbirds fly
guilty from a dawn haul
of fallen fruit. We too
breakfast on sweetnesses.

Soon plum trees will be bone,
grown delicate with frost's
formalities. Their black
angles will tear the snow.

Balsam

Balsam impatiens. 'Leaves
oval, slightly toothed. Flowers
five-petalled with a full lip,
a hood and spur of silk.'

On this slow autumn day
the apple branches lean
against the ground, the white
seeds ripen privately
in the apple's darkness.

Noli me tangere
wild in the damp of the wood.
The pods explode in my hand
as the beat of a trapped
animal there, the seed
on my palm. The hawsers
of the pod recoil, greens
never seen before, damp
silks worn new, still shaking.

Himalayan balsam: 'found
in stony places, secretly,
especially by streams.'

Buzzard

No sutures in the steep brow
of this cranium, as in mine
or yours. Delicate ellipse
as smooth as her own egg

or the cleft flesh of a fruit.
From the plundered bones on the hill,
like a fire in its morning ashes,
you guess it's a buzzard's skull.

You carry it gently home,
hoping no Last Day of the birds
will demand assembly
of her numerous white parts.

In the spaces we can't see
on the other side of walls
as fine as paper, brain and eye
dry out under the gossamers.

Between the sky and the mouse
that moves at the barley field's
spinning perimeter, only
a mile of air and the ganging

crows, their cries stones at her head.
In death, the last stoop, all's risked.
She scorns the scavengers
who feed on death, and never

feel the lightning flash of heart
dropping on heart, warm fur, blood.

Ram

He died privately.
His disintegration is quiet.
Grass grows among the stems of his ribs,
Ligaments unpicked by the slow rain.
The birds dismantled him for spring nests.
He has spilled himself on the marsh,
His evaporations and his seepings,
His fluids filled a reservoir.
Not long since he could have come
Over the Saddle like a young moon,
His cast shadow whitening Breconshire.

The blue of his eye is harebell.
Mortality gapes in the craters of his face.
Buzzards cry in the cave of his skull
And a cornucopia of lambs is bleating
Down the Fan of his horns.
In him more of October than rose hips
And bitter sloes. The wind cries drily
Down his nostril bones. The amber
Of his horizontal eye
Is light on reservoir, raven
In winter sky. The sun that creams
The buzzard's belly as she treads air
Whitens his forehead. Flesh
Blackens in the scrolls of his nostrils,
Something of him lingering in bone
Corridors catches my throat.

Seeking a vessel for blackberries and sloes
This helmet would do, were it not filled
Already with its own blacks,
Night in the socket of his eye.

From Clarence Bridge, Newport

Esk. Isca. Usk. Every day
mud sculpted to fresh form,
river-grain breaking, according
to the tide, tentatively,
violently at the stone feet
of the bridge. This afternoon
gulls cry under the arches, white
as wreaths of effluent,
plastic, feathers which turning tides
lay at the monument. No one
waits here. Wind bandages my mouth.
From melting snows of Ebbw,
Honddu, Usk, Sirhowy
processions of icy air
file to the sea, threading under
and over the bridges crying
a hymn of wind and water.

Heron at Port Talbot

Snow falls on the cooling towers
delicately settling on cranes.
Machinery's old bones whiten; death
settles with its rusts, its erosions.

Warning of winds off the sea
the motorway dips to the dock's edge.
My hands tighten on the wheel against
the white steel of the wind.

Then we almost touch, both braking flight,
bank on the air and feel that shocking
intimacy of near-collision,
animal tracks that cross in snow.

I see his living eye, his change of mind,
feel pressure as we bank, the force
of his beauty. We might have died
in some terrible conjunction.

The steel town's sulphurs billow
like dirty washing. The sky stains
with steely inks and fires, chemical
rustings, salt-grains, sand under snow.

And the bird comes, a surveyor
calculating space between old workings
and the mountain hinterland, archangel
come to re-open the heron-roads,

meets me at an inter-section
where wind comes flashing off water
interrupting the warp of the snow
and the broken rhythms of blood.

Mrs Frost

Turning my head a moment
from the geriatrics' ward
I see the bare wood bowed
quietly under the rain,
mists rising in silence.

Her white head is lowered
to her one good shaking hand,
clear thoughts rising from a body
ninety-two years old and done-for,
waiting to look up, blue, blind,

from another century
when I stop reading. Portia
perfectly remembered, just
and gentle in her mind and mine.
The undiscriminating rain

brisk as nurses, chills the wood
to the bone as night comes on.
In the beaded silks of rain
the trees feed secretly
while she, not sleeping, remembers.

Ice Queen

This girl holds me at heart's distance
with the stare of her grey eyes.
She defies me with a brow's flicker
and the angle of elbow and hip.

Yesterday it snowed. For a while
it was perfect. Over the white lawn
the clothes line curved in exact ellipse.
Suddenly a blackbird dropped on the rope
like a male dancer, and snow
fell on snow cutting a furrow
precise as its own shadow.
Then the grit lorries came and sleet
pitted the whiteness. Yesterday's snow
over her shoulder drips from the eaves
and abruptly slides from the roof.

The coldness casts perfectly its
shadow from one face to the other.
She falters. I am cut by the snow's soft lash.

Suicide on Pentwyn Bridge

I didn't know him,
the man who jumped from the bridge.
But I saw the parabola
of long-drawn-out falling in the brown

eyes of his wife week after week
at the supermarket cash-out.
We would quietly ask 'How is he?'
hear of the hospital's white

care, the corridors between her
and the broken man in the bed,
and the doctors who had no words,
no common supermarket women's talk.

Only after the funeral
I knew how he'd risen, wild
from his chair and told her
he was going out to die.

Very slowly from the first leap
he fell through winter, through the cold
of Christmas, wifely silences,
the blue scare of ambulance,

from his grave on the motorway
to the hospital, two bridges down.
A season later in a slow cortège
he has reached the ground.

Welsh Blacks

The cattle come to the hedge,
curious and hopeful, their hay
a mess on the snow. Six Welsh Blacks
and their bull slowly approaching
over the perfect field. Each tree
remarkable against snow,
an illustration from the book
of winter. Frozen waters fall
down the face of the Fan and fringe
the frontal bones of the bull.
His red tongue flares in the hay.

Snow obliterates our tracks
and melts in the pulled sweetness
of hay on the cattle's breath.
The snow crosshatches where the corn
grew slant in summer.

Beyond silence an iron wind
begins, and a heavier snow
fills the ribcage and the kettle
of the skull. How can you, or he
in the black bulk of his beauty,
know what blizzard filled a kitchen
with goosefeathers and the whiff
of burning spirits the day
before a funeral? Or hear
the thunder of a secret snow
fall from a warm roof?

On Rhiwbina Hill

Often in winter I think of this
a car parked crookedly beside a wall,
track under snow and all the quiet trees
in the dead slow of winter. Everything
aslant the path cut into the slope,
boots gathering clay and dead leaves.
A branch of beech buds blossoming snow.
Children ringing like birds. A distant train
howled as it climbed, caught in its narrow track.

Underneath, in the dead distant fibres
of the reaching trees, something already
must have begun to live, unrecognized,
before the train had crossed the viaduct.
Already the severed beech twigs stirred
in my hands, veins spreading, finding sap, blood.

Shadows in Llanbadarn

All shadows on the wall are blue.
Ladder-shadow. The rope askew
on the tenth rung. The Manx kitten
leaping the gap to the orchard wall.
Yours, searching the February soil
for points of green. Papery brown
flowers of dead hydrangeas stir.

From the wall to the tenth rung
the kitten drops and settles, fur
black and tiger-barred with black,
tense at the rope a breath scares.
In her face the sudden sticky green
of buds in darkness burns with sun.
Your shadow turns. I hear it on the stair.

The ladder's last. The falling sun
gradually drowns it, rung by rung.

A Journal from France

Poems from Aubas, September 1979

September 9th

Somewhere in France (although I was navigator
I have no idea where it was)
we stopped the car on the straight road
running white between the tall corn.

We turned into a lane, a corridor
dividing the heat, marking its darknesses
with trees. There in the grass we picnicked.
There I was happy and you were not.

We had no names for the strange trees,
butterflies, the black and yellow spider
that ate the flies we startled into its trap.
In the silence we heard only swallows
and the hoarse, dry voice of the corn.

Later on that silent journey,
when I had forgotten how to be happy
so easily, and miles of innocent maize
had darkened in their own decay,
a red kite shadowed us.

Tonight in Aubas I can't sleep
listening for the shriek of the kite.
About us in the hot, dark fields
each sunflower, chin on clavicle,
blackens, scorched in its own flames.

The Village

The car, an open boat, fills up with heat.
Instinctively we stop, both reaching
for cameras. A red-roofed village
across two fields. One ploughed. One ready
for harvest. The field of maize

raised tall as a full sea,
green whitening in a long roll.
Beyond, the village is an island,
a crown, golden-walled, red-roofed.

More intimately it is woodsmoke;
a ladder leaning on a gleam of straw
and, in the grass, spilt, glistening
seed of a picnic melon.

La Cirque de Paris

Lion and lioness and two cubs
in a truck at Terrason.
Their faces like the sun
scorch the eyes of the watchers.
'Blood,' they say, for our cameras.

The river Vézère is drifting
the water-weed of its mane
against the bridge. Dust
cracks the throat of the megaphone.
The lions are closing their eyes.

Father and sons curl back
to their own golden-eyed dark.
But the lioness beats down
her hatred as the red sun sets
on so much shabbiness.

Seamstress at St. Léon

As we eat crushed strawberry ice
under a bee-heavy vine
we watch for the seamstress to come.
Through the open doorway we hear
her chatter, see her Singers
glint with gold roses in the dark room.

Embroidery cloths abandoned
at the roadside table; a weir
of lace falls from her chair; silks
spill blossoming from a basket.
Under its turning ribbon of gauze
her tea cools in a white cup.

She sings in the dark interior.
From the sills of the gardenless house
fuchsia and geranium blaze.
Her windows are framed with French knots,
the cracks seeded with lazy daisy.
Her rubber plant reaches the eaves.

Nothing troubles the afternoon dust
or breaks the tenor of bees
but her counterpoint. Out of sight
in their web of scaffolding
under the bridge, workmen whistle
and a hammer rings over water.

A fan of shadow slowly includes us.
Her tea is cold. Imperceptibly
the thicket of roses grows closer.
We make out the sinuous gilding
of sewing machines, vine leaves, stems
and iron tendrils of their treadles.

Lace glimmerings at dusk. A foam
of linen, flowers, silences.
Sunlight has flowed from her sills
of yellow stone. Bats are shuttling
their delicate black silks to mesh
that dark doorway on her absence.

Kingfishers at Condat

Our hair still damp from swimming,
heads full of deep brown water
reflecting with reeds, we drink
an apéritif in Condat.

At the heart of the village silence
of gold-dust and evening heat
the café is full of youths
in leather for motor-cycling.

Their bikes wait in the courtyard,
blue as mallard, glittering flies
taking nourishment from dust,
at rest from their buzzing and fuss.

Excluded, uneasy at their stares
and the outbreak of laughter, we carry
our drinks outside, read their newspaper
in revenge, like a bill of right.

Out here on the parapet
the stone has absorbed September.
We sit alone, sweetnesses
of the wine on our mouth and fingers.

Their laughter is distant. The river
moves its surfaces, its reedy
stirrings and sudden glitter
rushing under the bridge.

Downstream the Coly, where we swam,
Meets the Vézère in a wide
confluence, deceivingly
cool under the evening's gold.

The yard is loud with boys. With us
for audience, one by one they go
roaring and glittering into the trees.
The river moves in peace, and there!

under the bank where it's dark, blue
as fire the kingfishers are hunting,
blue as storm, iridescent, alive
to the quoit on the surface

where the fish rises. Dragonfly
blue crackling down the dark vein
of the riverbank, as quick
and as private as joy.

Rouffignac

In the forest overhead
summer fruit is falling
like the beat of a drum.

Hold your breath and you hear
millennia of water
sculpting limestone.

The river runs in the heat
of the sun. We are walking
in its grave, imagine

a throat choking with water,
a power drill at work. Vast
cupolas prove its turbulence.

I am not deceived
by the nursery frieze
of mammoth. The circus act

brings on the bison,
black and ochre
ponies on terra cotta.

The Vézère is a ghost,
its footprints everywhere.
Even the kitchen taps

run cloudy into the palms
of our hands, fill our mouths
with chalk.

Font de Gaume

Fourteen thousand years make little difference.
Some of us, finding smooth places in the rough
must carve there, using old water marks.
A stalactite for a horse's thigh, its eye
a fault, or where the river fingered a whorl
a vortex turned the doorways of the skull.
Sinews of calcite, muscles run and slack,
the belly droops, a boulder marbles bone.

The imagination's caverns cry for symbols,
shout to the hot sun in the present tense.
We walk again in the afternoon,
watch out for vipers lazy on their stones.
Two tractors are towing home the harvest.
Tobacco saps evaporate in rows.
The glittering Vézère is at its work,
its inexhaustible calligraphy.

Brother, grinding your colours by tallow light,
I hear your heart beat under my collarbone.

Les Combarelles

These are our thoughts,
the pulse in bone,
the stream in the artery.
We were young here,
made our first fires,
saw by tallow light
each other's skin
and astonished eyes.
Hieroglyphics,
words flowered, calcite
crusted to first poems.
We made a doe, drinking
at this natural stream.
It was not quite what we meant,
but a beginning, a source.

'Summer's going quickly now'

We are caught in a storm, this last day
at St. Amand de Coly. First rain
comes fast. It is suddenly cold.
In the café opposite the church
the old woman, almost blind, insists
we want apricot juice after all.
If she could see the glasses I am sure
she would polish them for us, proudly,
with an immaculate cloth. My French
scarcely adequate for the long, sweet
conversation she wants of us,
I tell her about Wales, our rain,
our language. Strangely she knows already.
A Welshman passed this way two days ago.
Hearing the thunder, rain at the open door,
she stands to feel it, reflectively.
'L'été va vite maintenant,' she says,
and again, no longer talking to us,
'L'été va vite maintenant.'

Notes

Letter From a Far Country
p. 9   Taid: 'grandfather'.
p. 10   Mamgu: 'grandmother' (South Wales).
        Pais: 'petticoat'.
p. 16   Nain: 'grandmother' (North Wales).
p. 17   Diaconydd: 'deacon'.
        Trysorydd: 'treasurer'.
p. 18   Mam iaith: 'mother tongue'.

Jac Codi Baw
p. 37   'Jac Codi Baw: 'Jack Dig Dirt': JCB.

Ram
p. 48   Saddle and Fan: parts of the Brecon Beacon mountains.